BEYOND STAIRS

2nd Edition

Professor Ouele

Beyond Stairs
Copyright © 2020 Professor Ouele

Library of Congress Control Number: 2020912671
ISBN-13: Paperback: 978-1-64749-172-7

All rights reserved. No part of this publication may be reproduced, distributed, or transmitted in any form or by any means, including photocopying, recording, or other electronic or mechanical methods, without the prior written permission of the publisher or author, except in the case of brief quotations embodied in critical reviews and certain other noncommercial uses permitted by copyright law.

Although every precaution has been taken to verify the accuracy of the information contained herein, the author and publisher assume no responsibility for any errors or omissions.No liability is assumed for damages that may result from the use of information contained within.

Printed in the United States of America

GoTo Publish

GoToPublish LLC
1-888-337-1724
www.gotopublish.com
info@gotopublish.com

BEYOND STAIRS

By the same author, to be published:

INTRODUCTION TO HANDICAPOLOGY

DEDICATED
TO ALL PERSONS WITH DISABILITIES
IN THE WORLD

ACKNOWLEDGEMENT

I express my heartfelt gratitude to all those who supported me in one way or another during the writing of this book.

NOTICE

When I write or sing, I do it with the aim of returning Africa to Africa and the world to the world. I do not point my finger at man, but at the evil hidden in him, in view of creating man.

The author

FOREWORD

In reading the pages that follow, the reader may think it is a fiction, a fairy tale, whereas it is an artistic rendition of facts that actually occur in the everyday lives of disabled individuals. Those disabled are often the victim of prejudice. People with disabilities are thought of as beggars, aggressors, good-for-nothing, sorcerers, etc... These prejudices erect a wall of misunderstanding between able-bodied people and people with disabilities, which hamper the socio-professional integration of the latter.

Despite the segregated environment that surrounds them, people with disabilities struggle to grab the place that they deserve in our society.

By placing himself at the antipodes of these prejudices, the disabled must redefine himself no longer as an under-man, but as a crucible of potential. The fight will not be easy. But the end is worth the effort.

The author

PREFACE

In this painful beginning of an unhappy century where pride, capitalism, and selfishness prevail over humanism and love of neighbor, offering a reflection on the theme "protection of the disabled" is senseless, if not to say illusory. All agree that the protection of minorities and the needy has faded. To see that, you just need to walk by shopping centers and along the boulevards of cities to see persons with disabilities abandoned to their sad fate, finding their pittance only by chance from the generosity of a few sensitive hearts. The persons with disabilities are surrounded by too many prejudices and constitute a multifaceted problem. Under the weight of suffering, the inferiority complex appears as a fatality, which forever closes the path of hope.

Abandoned by the government and often by their own social environment and family, the persons with disabilities have no other hope than their begging and their prayer, as if to say that the biblical thought "love one another" was for another age and other distant societies. "Each for himself and God for all," this seems to be the response of society to the injunctions of people with disabilities. This problem has other meanings: it is an issue of conscience for the social elite and an insult to human dignity.

Since the disabled persons are condemned to live, Professor Ouele invites them to their own care: "disabled persons help yourselves and heaven will help you": because beyond the negative prejudices, beyond pessimism, the author devotes all his life, time, financial means, and know-how to bring these people together, convincing them that while continuing tirelessly the fight for their rights, they must force themselves to realize that they carry within them great divine potentialities which doze and which they ignore.

Perfect Conscience SIPOWA (poet)

EPISODE ONE: Sosata (Pouneaboh's mother); Bobnoue (Sosata's girlfriend)

Pouneaboh and Sosata meet in the courtyard. Sosata observes Pouneaboh for a long time and realizes that he is paralyzed. She touches her child's feet from time to time and utters a monologue.

Sosata

More than two years have passed since Pouneaboh was born. Albert, his father, never came to visit. We have to admit that there are some evil men. If time were reversible, if I could become a youth again, I would avoid going with any man, regardless of his beauty or wealth. I should have thrown this offspring in a trashcan or in the latrine like others do. I kept him in the hope that he will go to school, become a great man, and shoulder me. Unfortunately, I realize he is disabled. A while ago, the World Health Organization, the Rotary, and the Government launched a massive, free vaccination campaign against poliomyelitis. Such campaign, greatly publicized by the media, lasted a few weeks. I did not heed it and the result is that Pouneaboh is paralyzed from the waist down. Poor me!

Bobnoue arrives quietly.

Bobnoue

What is going on, Sosaa? You look sad.

Sosata

I am tormented by Pouneaboh's problem.

Bobnoue

Pouneaboh! What is the matter with him?

Sosata

He is disabled.

Bobnoue

Disabled? How do you know?

Sosata

He is not walking, and he is over two years old. His legs are visibly atrophied.

Pouneaboh starts crying, as if he understands what his mother is saying about him. Bobnoue picks him up to console him.

Bobnoue

It is sad! I am a bit theistic. According to our religion, no soul disappears. When someone dies, his or her soul is reincarnated in the body of a living being. The soul of lepers, of the visually impaired, of the persons with muscular dystrophy, of the quadriplegics, of all disabled persons is the soul of people who were very evil in the past and come back to pay for their sins with atrocious suffering.

Sosata

Is that theosophy?

Bobnoue

As you wish!

Sosata

You scare me with your statements, Bobnoue. What can we do to wipe out his sins?

Bobnoue

Listen, Sosata! We cannot cancel history. But special prayers to God may improve the situation a little.

Sosata

Do you know how to word such prayers?

Bobnoue

Not really. It is up to those who have a lot of faith and who have had a certain initiation. Nonetheless, since the world is also made of mysteries, I think you could check with Tchengom.

Sosata

Who is Tchengom?

Bobnoue

Tchengom! Everybody knows him!

Sosata

Frankly, I do not know him.

Bobnoue

Tchengom is the greatest witch doctor; I mean the greatest thaumaturge of this village.

Sosata

Can you tell me where he lives?

Bobnoue

Of course, I can! He is two rivers from here. After the crossroads "sorcerer," you can see his house on the right. It is the only fenced-in house there.

Sosata

I am immensely grateful. Tomorrow, I will go to him with Pouneaboh.

Bobnoue

The day is already far advanced. I must leave you.

She goes into the room where Pouneaboh fell asleep.

Sosata

I will go with you.

Bobnoue

You do not need to. Good night, Sosata!

Sosata

You too.

Sosata makes her bed. During this time, some questions fill her mind:

Professor Ouele

The city of Pedago, not far from here, has a rehabilitation center for the physically disabled. Should we go there? Or should we go to Tchengom instead? I am in a quandary, but night will bring me advice.

She turns the light off and falls asleep.

END OF EPISODE ONE

EPISODE TWO: Sosata, Tchengom, Pouneaboh.

Sosata decides to go see Tchengom and arrives there early in the morning.

Sosata

Good morning, Tchengom!

Tchengom

Good morning, madam. What is the issue that brought you here so early in the morning?

Sosata

I am concerned with my son's problem.

Tchengom

Ok! Speaking of your son, I need to tell you the truth: he is not like the other children. He is very complicated. Pouneaboh, I think that is his name …

Sosata surprised:

Sosata

Incredible! It actually is his name.

Tchengom

As I was saying, Pouneaboh is very complicated: he has four eyes.

Sosata

But I only see two!

Tchengom

It is normal. The other two can be seen only by the initiated, like me. He will never grow. If he continues to live, it is because death refuses him. If you kill him, he will come back in your next pregnancy, unless you decide not to procreate.

Sosata is so scared that she lays Pouneaboh on the floor. He is crying, but she no longer wishes to touch him.

Sosata

What can I do to get rid of this little devil?

Tchengom

Listen! I am the only one, yes, the only one in this village qualified to help you. I am not a charlatan. All I ask of you is to give me 80.000 francs.

Sosata

Where am I going to find 80.000 francs in these difficult times?

Tchengom

Your choice! I want to make it clear that this charge is set; I cannot change it.

Sosata

Excuse me for a moment, please.

She summons her courage; she takes Pouneaboh and ties him on her back using her loincloth. She leaves with her son, walks away from Tchengom's hut, and monologues:

This man is smart. I just earned 80.000 francs yesterday at the tontine. I have to give it to him; he will help me.

She unravels part of her loincloth, takes the sum that Tchengom had asked for, and goes back to see him.

… The sum I am giving you is all I own.

Tchengom

(Gravely)

If you regret giving this, I will return it. Take it and go back home with your Lucifer!

             Sosata

No, no, I beg you!

             Tchengom

Well! … If you preserve this child, he will end up giving you death.

             Sosata

Rid me of this devil, I beg you.

Pouneaboh cries inconsolably. In the meantime, Tchengom shakes some old calabashes and takes some stones from them. He also takes an ointment handy.

             Tchengom

Here! Swallow this stone immediately. On your way back home, pass by the Toben forest. When you are sure that no one is watching, spread this ointment all over yourself (he gives it to her), abandon this devil under a tree, and flee. Do you understand?

             Sosata

Yes, Tchengom.

             Tchengom

That is all. You may go.

             Sosata

Goodbye, Tchengom.

             Tchengom

Goodbye, madam.

Sosata follows Tchengom's instructions. Pouneaboh, abandoned under a tree, cries. He cries desperately.

END OF EPISODE TWO

EPISODE THREE: Djenvum (the hunter), Fo (village chief), Pouneaboh (Djogo), the director of the orphanage [female].

Djenvum goes hunting.

> Djenvum
>
> It is only nine o'clock and the heat is already unbearable. I had planned to check all my traps at 6 AM before going hunting, but unfortunately, I was still a hostage of fatigue. I have to pass by the very first trap. The animals have become sly, and do not let you catch them easily anymore.
>
> Look! A partridge struggling in the trap. It is certainly mine.

He runs, catches it, and finishes it off.

> Poor partridge, I will eat you tonight, with my family. I imagine that other traps kept away hedgehogs and porcupines. I am encouraged and I shall check them all, right away.

He walks fast, but suddenly hears the cry of a baby and wonders:

> Why would a woman come with her child in this brush, under this unbearable sun?

This child cries insistently. Djenvum is confused and starts looking for him.

> Djenvum
>
> Oh Jesus, help! A child abandoned in the middle of the bush!

He picks him up, tries to console him, but in vain.

> Is there a greater crime than such an act? Devil women; why treat this child who did not choose to be born this way? The unhappiness of some

women, however, is that they have not been able to procreate. Where should I take him? ... One solution comes to mind. I should take him to Fo, the village chief, who is also the officer of vital statistics.

He comes out of the brush with the child and goes to Fo.

Good morning, Your Majesty!

Fo

Good morning! Do you have a problem?

Djenvum

Yes, Your Majesty. I bring you a child. I found him abandoned under a tree as I was hunting.

Fo

Do you have any information about him?

Djenvum

No, Your Majesty.

Fo

I have cases like this regularly. It is difficult for us to know the name of this child; therefore, please suggest me a name by which we can call him from now on.

Djenvum

I suggest we call him Djogo.

Fo

Djogo! Does this name have a special meaning for you?

Djenvum

Yes, Your Majesty. Djogo means a person who is suffering. This name conveys the state of suffering in which I found him.

Fo

Your suggestion is accepted. He must be about two. Could we go downtown and leave him at the Nouepepon Orphanage?

Djenvum

Your Majesty, I am very dirty.

Fo

In this case, we can separate. I need to go with him now, right after completing his birth certificate.

Djenvum

Goodbye, Your Majesty!

Fo

Goodbye…

Fo drives Djogo to the orphanage.

Good morning, madam director!

The director

Good morning, sir. I am listening.

Fo

I bring you a child who was abandoned in the brush. He was found this morning by a hunter.

The director

Another abandoned child! Of the thirty children I adopted, twenty were abandoned by their mothers. Women increasingly throw away or kill their children. More and more women throw away or kill the children they give birth to. I wonder what this kind of women will say to God. They do not know that they are committing crimes in the same way as those who poison or stab. May I identify you, sir?

Fo

Why not? I am the chief of Naam village. I am also the officer of vital statistics.

The director

Good. I suppose you gave a name to this child.

Fo

Yes. His name is Djogo. I'll give you his birth certificate. Do you have other questions?

The director

No.

Fo

Goodbye, madam.

The director

Goodbye, sir.

END OF EPISODE THREE

EPISODE FOUR: Mefo (Medefo's girlfriend), the director of the orphanage, Djogo.

Seven years later, Djogo has grown a lot. He speaks very well and can move with the help of crutches. He has fun with his friends.

Unfortunately, the economic crisis is affecting the orphanage to such an extent that it will be closing.

                Mefo

Medefo is expecting me. Nonetheless, I need to hear this latest news.

            VOICE ON THE RADIO

The director of the Nouepepon Orphanage is informing the public that the center will be closing in the next few days because of the profound financial difficulties it is experiencing. Therefore, she is appealing to all people of goodwill who would like to adopt the children to come by her office after hearing this communiqué.

Mefo runs to Medefo and knocks at her door.

                Medefo

Who is it?

                Mefo

Open the door.

She goes in.

                Medefo

What news do you bring me?

Mefo

I just heard the news of the upcoming closing of the Nouepepon Orphanage. The director of this center would like some families to welcome the children. I am puzzled.

Medefo

It is pretty good news! Let us take a tour. Marriage never meant much to me. But I love children. I could adopt one of those orphans.

They hail a taxi and go to the orphanage.

Medefo and Mefo

Good morning, director!

Director

Good morning.

Medefo

We heard the announcement of the closing of this center and we came for the orphans.

Director

The announcement has been running for a week. The orphans were about thirty initially; however, only one is left. His name is Djogo. Just a moment, please.

She leaves to go get Djogo. Mefo sees him and starts whispering:

Mefo

Look, Medefo! He is paralyzed. What will you do with a disabled child? I suggest you leave him. It is certainly because he is paralyzed that no one wanted to take him. If you adopt him, he will be a useless burden on you.

> Medefo

Nevertheless, let us be human. I have to take him, be as it may.

The director arrives with Djogo.

> The director

Well! Here he is. His name is Djogo.

> Medefo

Djogo, how are you?

> Djogo

I am fine.

> Medefo

Do you want to come home with me?

> Djogo

Yes.

> The director

What is your name and what do you do, madam?

> Medefo

My name is Medefo. I am a pediatrician at the Talen Central Hospital.

The director takes note of the information that Medefo provided.

> The director

Djogo, you will live with her from now on. Do you understand?

> Djogo

Yes, madam.

> The director

Here is his birth certificate. He attended preparatory school at this center and is going to first grade. He started school late because of his physical disability. But he expresses himself very well in French and is intelligent. You may go.

Medefo

Goodbye!

They leave the director's office. Mefo's mood has changed: she is visibly concerned by Medefo's decision.

Mefo

I will join you. I need to run an errand.

Medefo

Where are you going precisely, since we have to go home together with this child?

Gravely.

Mefo

It does not matter where I am going.

Medefo

You have had a frown on your face for a few minutes. Can you tell me what is wrong?

Mefo

…

Medefo

I guess you are upset by my decision to adopt Djogo.

Mefo

Now we understand each other. Of course, you will never see me at your house again. Goodbye!

She hails a taxi and leaves.

> Medefo
>
> My best friend leaves me just because I decided to adopt a disabled child. The world is incredible. My decision is made. I will not change it.

She hails a taxi and goes home with Djogo. They are at home.

> Medefo
>
> Here we are. I am now your mother, do you understand, Djogo?
>
> Djogo
>
> Yes, Mother.

She brings him something to eat. He utterly enjoys it.

> Medefo
>
> I will do everything to ensure your happiness. You will be a happy child. Tomorrow, I will enroll you at the Pompom Public School. Then, with the diploma, you can get a job and earn your living.

Djogo smiles.

> Now that you've finished eating, I will take you to bed so you do not get too tired.

She takes him to bed.

> Good night, Djogo!
>
> Djogo
>
> Good night, Mother.

END OF EPISODE FOUR

EPISODE FIVE: Medefo, Djogo, the director of Pompom Public School

Medefo
Good morning, Djogo. Did you sleep well?

Djogo
Yes, Mother.

Medefo
The sun is already up. In this back-to-school period, we need to go very early and be the first at the door of the director, or else, we will wait a long time, with little chance of being seen. Let us go.

They get ready and hail a taxi to go to Pompom Public School.

Look! The school is already crowded with parents and schoolchildren. Despite our early start, we will not be able to be served first, as we had hoped.

The director arrives. The stampede intensifies. Medefo painfully hauls Djogo. The first people in line allow her to stand in front of them so as to be served first. The selection starts: Medefo is called by the director:

The director of Pompom
Good morning, madam! What can I do for you?

Medefo
Good morning, director. We come from Kebissi…

The director
I do not want to know where you are coming from. Be brief and clear.

Medefo
I would like to enroll my child in this school, first grade.

The director

How old is your child?

Medefo

He is nine years old.

The director

Madam, this child is too old to attend the first grade in my school. You may try your luck elsewhere.

Medefo

Sir, he did not attend school early because of his physical disability …

The director

So…?

Medefo

Could you, please, grant him an age waiver?

The director

What is an age waiver?

Medefo

An age waiver simply means that, without considering the age of this child, you will enroll him in your institute.

The director

Why, madam?

Medefo

Sir, this age waiver would allow this physically disabled child to regain lost time, to get an education like the other children. You know very well that a person with disabilities with an education is one less beggar on the streets.

The director

Madam, you mistake my education institute for a social service. You waste time for all the other parents whom I need to see. Go elsewhere.

He gets up, calls the second parent, and makes Medefo leave with Djogo. They leave profoundly disappointed.

Medefo

This is too bad. There are no more schools close to our home. You will need to stay home.

Djogo is sad.

Djogo

Waaaa, Mom!

Medefo

Calm down, Djogo. Failure is sometimes a stepping-stone to success. Here is what I suggest: I can use the money that would have been paid for your education and the books to buy you a tricycle and a wheelchair. Then, I will save money to enroll you in a European school when you're older. What do you think?

Djogo

I agree, Mom. That is well thought out.

They hail a taxi for the store where they do all their shopping. They hire a van which transports them home with the purchased devices. As soon as they arrive, Djogo starts wheeling around in his wheelchair. His mother observes him and encourages him. Here and there, he smiles at her with gratitude.

Medefo

Now you can move with less difficulty.

While he continues wheeling around, she goes to the kitchen to quickly prepare the meal.

Djogo!

Djogo

Mother!

Medefo

Dinner is ready. Come to the table.

Djogo sits and eats with pleasure. He is then sleepy and leaves his dinner. Medefo takes him to his room and puts him to bed. She is also sleepy and falls asleep.

END OF EPISODE FIVE

EPISODE SIX: Several years have passed. Medefo and Djogo are at home.

Medefo

I was able to enroll you in a French school. I have to tell you, it wasn't easy. We only need to take care of the last formalities for your departure.

Djogo

Thank you, Mom. May our dream become reality!

Medefo

A workshop for pediatricians is taking place today in Robono and it will last all day. I was invited. Therefore, I need to leave you for a moment, Djogo. Before going, I am arranging things so that you will have all you may need. Here is the piano so that you can entertain yourself. You can also listen to the radio, which is right here, and food is in the refrigerator.

Djogo

Thank you, Mom, for all that you have done for my happiness. How will you get there?

Medefo

I will drive. I will drive by the highway.

Djogo

Mom, I have bad feelings about that: do not drive on the highway. Many people were killed on it. Almost every day a family mourns a loved one. I suggest you take the train.

Medefo

It is true that the highway has already swallowed many souls. But it is also true that many people have driven on it safely; why can't I be among these?

Djogo *(anguished)*

Hm!

> Medefo

See you soon, Djogo.

> Djogo

See you soon, Mom.

Left alone, Djogo cannot let go of his anguish. Nevertheless, he tries to move about the house in his wheelchair. He also plays some piano. The more time goes by, the more his anguish increases. With difficulty, he finishes a small apple he took from the refrigerator. It is 11:00 PM, and Medefo has not come back. Right at the time when Djogo turns on the radio, he hears this news:

> Voice on the radio
>
> On the Robondo road, an accident took the lives of the following persons:
>
> -Amadou, a part-time lecturer at the University of Emoua;
>
> -Nouemo Blaise, an agronomist with the Department of Agriculture at Dom;
>
> -and Medefo, a pediatrician at the Talen Central Hospital. The victims' families should come to the Zupok Hospital morgue to pick up the bodies.

Djogo explodes in tears.

> Djogo
>
> Oh, Mom! If only you had heeded my advice, you could have escaped this tragedy. Here I am without support, like a rootless tree, which may fall at any time. Poor me.

END OF EPISODE SIX

EPISODE SEVEN: Djogo, passers-by (John, Peter, Tamo, Somo)

After a few weeks, Djogo is in the street, in front of a pharmacy. He is seated on a mat and is holding a plate that he shows 1to all passers-by to beg. He monologues.

Djogo

I am incessantly chased by a sad fate. I know little of what happiness is; when it haunts me, it only lasts the blink of an eye. I never met my parents. The economic crisis cut my stay at the Nouepepon Orphanage. Mother Medefo was my guardian angel: she brought me to the threshold of glory, but unfortunately, she passed away too soon. Here I am, made a beggar to survive.

His screams are pitiful:

Aaa…aaa…aaaa… so close to glory, and yet pushed back to the lowest rung of the ladder. What a sad destiny. Aaaa… I am so miserable! Help me.

John walks by Djogo without giving him anything. After a few steps, he goes back toward him.

John

Here, I only have 500 francs to give you.

Djogo screams with happiness.

Djogo

Ah! Thank you, one thousand times, thank you. May God bless you!

John disappears. Djogo sees Peter and starts his misery chant again:

Djogo

Aaaa… aaaa… babialaaa… salaka… Mokuita, pewekuiteaa… I am so miserable, so very miserable; help me, please. You are certainly rich; can you give me some money? Aaa…

Peter

You obviously want to ask me for some money. Too bad for you if you are poor! I prefer that my money be stolen from me, rather than offer it to a disabled. You, the disabled, are mean, good-for-nothing, and mischievous.

Djogo

Waah! Why was I born? What sin did I commit for being what I am, Lord? God, you should not have created me… You seem proud of not being handicapped. It is people of your ilk who are largely responsible for our way of acting. In front of us, you often feel superior, you display contempt and antipathy. You say we are mischievous. Look at the mentally challenged: they are quiet in certain environments; but, in others, they are furious. They walk with stones, and they are ready to hit in the head anyone who approaches them. It is because you irritate them. Some of you spit on the leprous when they walk by. How do you expect them to react?

Peter

Your words will not make me give you alms…

Djogo

In any case, continue your way. If you do not want to help me, do not stop others from doing it.

Peter leaves. Djogo sees another passer-by and resumes his chant

Allaa, mokuitaa, mokuitaa, miserable, yes, I am miserable. Who can help me?

Tamo is already very close to Djogo. The latter grabs Tamo's pants so as to attract his attention more.

Please, sir, a little money to eat. Have mercy. I have not eaten anything since morning. I have no parents.

Tamo

Can you leave the passers-by alone? You upset me. You clutter up the passage just like a bunch of garbage. The municipality should think of picking you up like trash. Anyway, take these 15 francs, poor wretch!

He disappears.

Djogo

… Thank you …

He is upset by the insult and nods his head negatively.

Ah… God, if you could re-create me, I would wish not to be disabled, a person on whom befall all the sins of the world. In short, disabled equals scapegoat!

Somo arrives. After recovering from the insult, Djogo continues to beg, as he could not help it.

I have no mother or father. My guardian died. I am miserable. Allaa…babiaa …kuita, kuita… please help me, I am disabled.

Somo

Disabled, disabled, what is it? The more you underestimate yourself, the more you thwart your talents. You are not as miserable as you think. Do not ignore the compensation phenomenon, according to which when one loses the use of an organ, another becomes stronger. As everyone, you have talents that need to be developed. You suffer the cold, the heat, and the insults, whereas they can be avoided. You penalize all disabled persons because through you, the public sees the rest.

A lot of volunteers want to help you, but first they want to see you at work. At that point, they will come to your help. You see, society is not mean. Some philanthropists could help you with 10. 000, 15. 000 francs, and even more. But for how long? Remember that a child to whom we give food is nourished for one day, but the child whom we teach how to prepare his meal is nourished for life.Begging is not a good thing. You want charity. But don't forget it diminishes you.

Stop crying, stop considering your infirmity as a curse. Some disabled people, like President Roosevelt, have governed the world by their ideas. Why not you too?

Djogo

Ah! Sir, your propositions comfort me.I was just dealing with the grave insults of the world before you arrived ...

Somo

Person with disabilities, get up!

Listen to the bell tolling:

Yes! This bell tolls for you.

You stayed a long time

in the hellish lethargy,

in apathy,

in gloom.

Person with disabilities, get up!

You often believed,

and still seem to believe,

that your paralyzed limbs,

your blurred eyes,

condemn you to inaction.

Person with disabilities, get up!

You can work, but do you know it?

You can counsel, but do you know it?

It is time you brought your contribution

for national construction.

Give up begging, jealousy, and laziness,

and discover the talents that are hidden in you!

Person with disabilities, get up!

Get up on your wheelchair.

Get up on your crutches.

Make your legs your support.

Get out of your solitude.

And together we will see, judge, and take action.

Djogo

By the power of your words, you have created in me a new man. May my tears dry! I want to work, I will work, and I will turn my life into a challenge. Enough is enough. But what can I do concretely?

Somo

There are a wide variety of jobs suited to your disability. There are disabled doctors, professors, tailors, shoemakers, the list goes on. I suggest you learn sculpture and serigraphy.

Djogo

Ok! Ok!

Somo

Without delay, I will take you to my friend Loko. He will train you.

They leave, headed to see Loko. As they go, they converse. Dogo is on his tricycle.

I would like us to be better acquainted. My name is Somo! What is yours?

Djogo

My name is Djogo.

Somo

My dear friend, the world of the disabled is a world almost lagging behind, yet you have a lot of potential. You have certain skills that so-called able-bodied people do not have. You just need to exploit them.

Society is partially responsible for your lagging behind because it does not take sufficient care of you. But you contribute to slowing down your integration into society: disabled persons interact just like the wives in a polygamist family: they are divided. The visually impaired have their world; the deaf have theirs, etc... and those worlds are not serene. If I may paraphrase Karl Marx, I would say: disabled people of the world unite!

Djogo

Your comment seems appropriate. Each one wants to stay in their own world. It is because of all the Byzantine quarrels that we face.

Somo

It will, however, be necessary to silence these sterile quarrels and create a united front among you. A united front is the best way to freedom. For example, you could create small businesses.

Djogo

Your ideas are very good. But where would we find the means to achieve such projects? In other words, aren't these stupendous?

Somo

It is nothing. I already told you that society is not made only of mean people. There are also philanthropists. They can help you, if your project is serious.

Disabled should all realize that they are full-fledged people ...

Djogo

On this, I cannot agree with you. A disabled person is not full-fledged: I never had the opportunity to study this in depth, but logically, I think that something whole is complete. An orange without one slice is no longer a whole orange. We can say that it is a whole orange minus a slice. The same is true for us: a one-eyed person is a whole person minus his eye; a deaf person is a whole person minus the hearing capacity. The assistance of the able-bodied is indispensable to us.

Somo

Are we not assisting you already by organizing national and international days in your honor?

Djogo

You make me think of the world lepers' day: certain people think they give gifts when they actually got rid of clutter. They offer ripped clothing or broken shoes. The gifts that are acceptable are diverted and never reach their consignees.

Somo

It is regrettable. Sorry, when I met you, you were saying that you have no mother or father, that your guardian died. How did it happen?

Djogo

I never met my father. I never met my mother. I was brought up in an orphanage and then by a guardian. and she died.

Somo

Where do you sleep?

Djogo

I do not have a stable place. At dusk, I put together some cardboard. I spread it in front of any store where I will spend the night. Sometimes, the night security guards come, scare me, and chase me away.

Somo gazes at Djogo with compassion.

You can sleep at my place. I live in the Vava neighborhood. As you arrive at the "Night Owls' Club," you will see a yellow house on your right. That is my house... here we are at my friend Loko's.

He knocks on the door.

Loko

Come in!

Somo

Good morning, Loko! I bring you an apprentice.

Loko

Good morning, Somo! I see that he is disabled.

Why are you bringing me an apprentice who is on the threshold of death? I do not like having disabled ...

Djogo is outraged and lifts his eyes to the sky.

Djogo

Heaven!

Somo

My friend, you certainly should not say such things. Djogo is obviously disabled, but he is not a pariah! If my observations are correct, everyone is disabled one way or another. As proof, I can say that the current economic crisis has disabled the whole world. We have to accept him as he is. You are content now to be physically sound; but, do you know what tomorrow may bring? If he behaves well, we need to make all efforts to support him instead of marginalizing him. I was forgetting to tell you something: it is better to be physically disabled and morally sound than being physically sound and morally disabled...

Djogo

Well said, Somo...

Somo

Djogo interrupted me when I also wanted to tell you that the world is in crisis today, I mean in deep crisis, because it is full of morally disabled people who need spiritual crutches. Selfish people want to have everything for themselves by creating a climate of rebellious injustice. Other people embezzle national funds to keep them in accounts abroad where they cannot be withdrawn when needed. Other people in whose veins flow tribalism and corruption crowd our offices and roads. Some eternal absentees only come to work at the end of the month to collect their pay stubs. Those people mentioned above are more disabled than Djogo. All who claim they are not disabled are only ignoring their illness.

Loko

Before the tribunal of my conscience, I am wrong and I apologize for the wrong I have committed toward Djogo.

He coughs to clear his voice.

Going back to the apprenticeship, which is the focus of our meeting, I usually accept a lump sum of 100.000 francs. To correct my fault, please give me only 60.000 francs.

Somo

This charge seems, to me, still high. We are going through hard times. Can you accept 50.000 francs?

Loko *(pensive)*

...No... I accept it quite exceptionally.

Somo takes a checkbook from his documents and signs a check.

Somo

Here is a check for 50. 000 francs.

Joy lightens up Djogo's face.

Loko

Thank you, Somo.

Loko takes the form for the apprenticeship contract from his drawer, fills it, and has Somo sign it.

Somo

I have to be in a meeting in the next few minutes, so I have to leave you, Djogo! Here is the key to the main door. You can go to the house whenever you want. Goodbye, Loko.

Loko

Goodbye, my good friend!

Djogo

See you soon, Somo.

Somo shakes hands with Loko, and then with Djogo and disappears.

Loko

We cannot start today, Djogo. I have to take you through the workshops and introduce you to the other apprentices. Tomorrow, at exactly 8 o'clock, you need to be here to start your training.

He comments on all the paintings.

Follow me. Look at these paintings. They were painted by other apprentices like you.

I am going to introduce to you those with whom you will be working. On your left is Nguetchom.

On your right, Paktcha. It is all for today. Did you understand?

Djogo

Yes.

Loko

I am your teacher. You should learn to address me saying "yes, sir."

Djogo

Yes, sir.

Loko

Goodbye.

Djogo leaves. He is seen later at home with Somo. Loko wants to go home too.

Nguetchom and Paktcha, where are you?

Nguetchom and Paktcha

We are here, sir!

Loko

It is time, go home.

They leave hastily. Loko leaves last, after closing everything.

END OF EPISODE SEVEN

EPISODE EIGHT: Djogo, passers-by, Loko, Paktcha, Nguetchom.

Djogo leaves home very early. He goes fast with his tricycle. At the foot of the hill, he is very tired and cannot continue by himself. He counts on any assistance (by passers-by).

> Djogo
>
> Good morning, sir. Can you give me a hand?
>
> Passerby 1
>
> I am tired.

He leaves without helping. Another one arrives.

> Djogo
>
> Good morning, sir.
>
> Passerby 2
>
> Good morning!

Without waiting to be asked, he pushes Djogo's tricycle while singing. He accompanies him to his training place. He arrives at the same time as his boss and the other apprentices. The passer-by leaves. Loko opens the workshop. All enter and get ready to start. He sits near Djogo.

> Loko
>
> We can start. Remember this: during your training, imitation is necessary.

Loko takes a pencil, some sheets, and makes some simple designs.

> Observe me first and then imitate me.

He gives Djogo some material, which he imitates and makes some beautiful drawings. Loko has Djogo undergo many imitation exercises and gives him more assignments, before going to inspect the work of the other apprentices. When he comes back, Djogo finishes his assignment.

>Very good, Djogo. Have you done this before?
>
>Djogo
>
>No, master.
>
>Loko
>
>You have some talent. Some apprentices went through this for two months without success. Now we are going to change the subject. We are going to start painting.

He teaches Djogo the matching of colors and the impression, and then he gives him a series of exercises, which he must do along with other apprentices. Once set up, Djogo works seriously. He talks softly:

>Djogo
>
>These exercises are more difficult than the ones I did before. However, I can make it. I am determined. I cannot go back now.

Djogo is visibly challenged, but he succeeds nonetheless. He finishes the paint before finishing his work and asks Paktcha to bring him a second tube of paint.

>Please, Paktcha, bring me the paint that is in front of you.

Severely.

>Paktcha
>
>What are you saying? Do you think I am your servant? You come and get it.
>
>Djogo
>
>Heaven! Yesterday, I was begging in order to have something to eat. Do I have to beg today as well to get assistance from my co-worker?

Nguetchom

No, Paktcha! You must not shake the morale of this boy. He is a disabled person. People like him have double suffering: they suffer physically and morally. Their moral suffering is often worse than the physical suffering. Your stance does not help his morale. I cannot understand why you want to compare a request for assistance to a form of servitude.

Nguetchom brings the paint to Djogo. In order to hide his shame, Paktcha pretends he is busy.

Djogo

Thank you, my friend.

Nguetchom

You are welcome. Be strong.

A moment later, Loko comes out of his office to check on the work of the apprentices. He admires the work done by Djogo and says:

Loko

It is extraordinary, Djogo! Here you are, already a good painter.

Joy spreads on Djogo's face. He smiles.

It is more than enough for today. Your very receptive intelligence made me do with you in one day what I do with others in several months. You can go home now.

Djogo

Goodbye, sir!

Loko

Goodbye! Nguetchom and Paktcha, you can go too.

Nguetchom and Paktcha leave the workshop. After that, Loko shuts the door and goes home.

ONE YEAR LATER

Djogo impresses his master and gets ahead of other apprentices. In his office, Loko whispers a monologue while the apprentices are at work.

> **Loko**
>
> Animated by a diabolical spirit, I almost refused to take in training the brave Djogo. He is the apprentice who has impressed me the most since I founded my business. He mastered his work very well and I think he already deserves a certificate for the completion of the training.

He calls Djogo

> Djogo, can you go get Somo? You deserve a certificate of completion for this training. I have to award it to you in his presence.
>
> **Djogo**
>
> Yes, sir, I can.

He goes happily and calls Somo who is resting at home.

> Somo, my master wants to award me the certificate of completion of the training. He needs you.
>
> **Somo**
>
> This news is very exciting. Let us go. Leave your tricycle. We are taking a taxi.

They go back to the training site and enter Loko's office.

> Loko

Good morning, Somo.

> Somo

Good morning, Loko. Long time no see.

> Loko

I called you here to give you Djogo's end of training certificate.

He awards it to him.

He really impressed me. I do not think I can teach him anything else. It is with sadness that I let him go.

> Somo

I can see his dynamism at home as well. I am well content with him.

Loko gets up, and shakes Djogo's and Somo's hands.

> Loko

Goodbye and good luck, Djogo.

Djogo and Somo leave. Loko accompanies them, comes back, and orders to close the workshop.

END OF EPISODE EIGHT

EPISODE NINE: Djogo (looking for a job), Somo, Ebobisse (secretary of Tayou & Sons Company), Donfack (Director of Carocam Enterprise), Koumkoum (chief of the personnel of Carocam), Tafo (secretary of Carocam Enterprise), Kala (Koumkoum's substitute), Tatou (Somo's brother), customers.

Djogo and Somo are at home

Somo

Djogo! Following your training, you need to look for a job. I will help you fill out some applications.

He takes some papers and writes two applications, which he gives to Djogo in an envelope:

Here are two job applications. Go and deliver them. Also, here is some money for transportation.

Djogo

Thank you.

He hands Djogo 2. 000 francs and Djogo leaves the house. After a few minutes, he is seen with a bag in his hands. He painfully climbs the stairs of the company to deliver his job application on the fourth floor. He runs into Secretary Ebobisse.

Good morning, madam!

Ebobisse

It is "miss." Good morning. How did you get to the fourth floor with your condition?

Djogo is sweating and visibly tired.

Djogo

As you can see, I got here with pockmarked feet. I tell you that this was for me the way of the Cross: more than a thousand steps, no elevator.

Ebobisse

What brings you here?

Djogo

On the radio, I heard that you have a vacancy for the position as a serigraph in this company. This is why I came to present my application.

Ebobisse

If you are the applicant, there is no need for you to give me the application. My boss gave me instructions: given the distance from the ground floor office, and due to the lack of an elevator, no disabled person can access this position.

Djogo

May I meet with your boss personally?

Ebobisse

Seeing him would not change anything. Since you insist, you can go. That is the door to his office.

Djogo knocks at Mr. Donfack's door.

Donfack

Come in!

Djogo enters. The director observes him.

Good morning. What can I do for you, sir?

Djogo

I am here for the job. In fact, I have…

Donfack interrupts him.

Donfack

Go back to my secretary. I gave her clear instructions in this regard. Goodbye, sir!

Djogo exits without saying a word and sees the secretary again.

Ebobisse

What did he say?

Djogo

Nothing good. However, there is something I do not understand: why are public buildings still inaccessible to the disabled? Is that not a blatant discrimination toward us? The Minister of Urban Development should think about the regulation regarding construction of public buildings. All these buildings should absolutely have elevators and ramps to allow disabled to move around.

Ebobisse

You just need to see him for this. Tell your minister also to create jobs for the disabled. I just followed my boss' orders.

Djogo

Thank you, goodbye.

Ebobisse

Goodbye, sir.

Djogo leaves the company visibly upset. He heads toward another one. He goes through the same process, with the difference that he only gets to the second floor. He explains his problem to Secretary Tafo.

Djogo

Good morning, sir!

Tafo

Good morning, what can I do for you?

Djogo

I come to present my job application.

Tafo

It is true that we are looking for a serigraph. But do you think you are fit for the job, with your disability?

Djogo

My disability is not an obstacle to my work. Test me to see what I am capable of.

Tafo leaves him in the waiting room for a few moments. He goes and explains the situation to his boss. The latter comes with a test.

Koumkoum

Good morning, sir. What is your name?

Djogo

Good morning. My name is Djogo.

Koumkoum

Well, Mr. Djogo, I will test you. If the result is satisfactory, I will hire you, or else...Take a seat and reproduce this portrait on a sheet of paper in one hour and a half.

Djogo sits. He is given all the necessary tools. Forty minutes later, he is done. He calls Koumkoum who is busy with other things.

Djogo

Please, sir, I'm done.

Koumkoum looks at his watch with surprise, takes Djogo's work, and appreciates it.

Koumkoum

You finished your assignment early, a good sign. Also, your work is impeccable. You are hired in our company.

Djogo

Thank you, sir.

Koumkoum

You should be proud of your performance. You know that in a company, what counts most is the performance. The social aspect comes after that. You will replace Kamdoum who left us to pursue his studies. He also was disabled. He had great working qualities: he was assiduous, hardworking, and focused. He got here in the morning and would not leave until the evening.

Djogo

This type of focus is a characteristic of almost all disabled persons. They may not have solid limbs to go pick up some beer at the bar or smoke a cigarette during business hours like the able-bodied. We stay at our workplace and we devote ourselves completely to our work. I am very flattered that a disabled person is being replaced by another in your company. This proves that you do not discriminate against us. But how can we convince all the other managers and company owners to do the same, especially to comply with the legislation relating to people with disabilities stipulating that at least 10% of the workforce of each company must be made up of people with disabilities?

Koumkoum

I consider disabled just as normal people. Those who marginalize them are wrong. They often do that because of ignorance. I also think that it is not that difficult for you to integrate in society. Disabled who have an opportunity to prove that they are as capable as the able-bodied should just defend themselves correctly, as you did, and just like your predecessor. This will convince many skeptics. We also need political will: if the government could use the same techniques that it uses to enforce payment of taxes, to impose that all respect the rights of disabled people, all would work fine. This was just an introduction. You can go back home now and come back in exactly one month to sign the contract and start working. I am going on a mission tomorrow, for three weeks. See you soon, Djogo.

A month later, Djogo goes back as planned.

Djogo

Good morning, Tafo.

Tafo

Good morning, sir.

Djogo

I have an appointment with your boss to sign my work contract.

Tafo

He was dismissed a few days ago. Go to his former office, you will find Mr. Kala who replaced him.

Djogo knocks on the door and enters.

Djogo

Good morning, sir.

Kala

…What is up, sir?

Djogo

I passed a test for the job as serigraph in your company. Mr. Koumkoum had told me to come today to start.

Kala

The decisions made by my predecessor only bind him. There is no vacancy in this company. I am sorry, sir.

Djogo

But...

Kala

Do not insist, sir. I am very busy.

Djogo leaves the office without saying anything more. In the main office, he says goodbye to Tafo. Far from the company, he monologues.

Djogo

I have no chance. Many people just like Kala adopt an attitude of rejection both to claim a bribe and to discourage the applicant and replace him with someone from their tribe.

A few moments later, Djogo is at home. He tells Somo.

I thought I would start working today. Unfortunately, the director who recruited me was dismissed and his replacement nullified his decisions.

Somo

Do not make it a huge issue. Most of the young graduates pass most of their time applying for a job instead of trying to create jobs. Instead of doing what one wants, one does what he can. I can leave you the premises I was thinking of renting. Eventually, I could help you buy the materials you need. The profits will be all yours. What do you think?

Djogo, happily.

Djogo

You are wise. The only problem may be assistance: if I need a heavy object or one that is far from me, I will need someone to help me.

Somo

Of course. Let us go so I can show you those premises.

They take a taxi to go to the premises. They walk around. After visiting the premises, they need to go buy the material:

Regarding the material, can you put together a list of the essentials?

Djogo

I will need some paint, some cloth, some wood, a few brushes …

Somo

Wait for me here. I will go get them. I will also get one of my little brothers who dropped out of school and now hangs out in the street. He will help you.

While he is away, Djogo wonders on his next endeavor. Somo comes back a few minutes later with the material and his little brother, and leaves right away:

Tatou, this is Djogo. You will assist him. Understood?

Tatou

Yes.

Djogo

I thank you, Somo, for your willingness and your availability.

Somo

You can thank the Lord. I have to leave you because in thirty minutes I need to be with my friends. Good luck to you all.

Djogo and Tatou

Thank you.

Djogo is very excited. He does not want to waste any time and gets to work right away. He practices drawing caricatures and printing them on cloth. Here and there, he asks Tatou for help.

> Djogo
>
> Can you please bring me the ream of papers that I see there on the paint container, Tatou?
>
> Tatou
>
> Yes, I am here to help you.

Tatou brings him the ream of papers. Djogo is very tired. He stops working.

> Djogo
>
> We can continue tomorrow.

Tatou shuts the windows and the door, and they go home. Many months later, Djogo has produced a lot of paintings and sculptures. He organizes an exhibit-sale in his workshop. Tatou is responsible for the set-up of the objects and surveillance. Djogo's workshop is full of curious people coming to see his masterpieces.

> First customer
>
> How much are these paintings?

He touches them.

> Djogo
>
> They are worth 25.000 francs each.
>
> First customer
>
> It is expensive for work produced by a disabled. If people like you could follow your example, life for them would be less difficult. Congratulations. Here is 50.000 francs, I will take two paintings.
>
> Djogo
>
> Thank you, sir.

>Second customer

How much do you charge for this painting and for this sculpture?

>Djogo

The painting is 25. 000 francs and the sculpted portrait 45. 000 francs. The total is only 70. 000 francs.

The second customer bursts out in laughter.

>Second customer

You are right to say "only." Your products are expensive. However, as an encouragement, I will not discuss the price. Here it is.

>Djogo

Thank you, sir.

>Second customer

Excuse me. I walked around your workshop and was struck by the fact that all the objects shown are made with great artistry. Are you really the author of all those paintings and sculptures?

>Djogo

Yes, I am, sir.

Second customer

It is marvelous. I congratulate you.

>Djogo

You flatter me.

>Second customer

All the best. Goodbye.

>Djogo

Thank you, sir.

Night is falling. Fewer visitors come and go. Tatou finds in it the excuse to go:

Tatou

Since customers are fewer, I can say that the exhibit is almost finished. Can I take a few minutes' break?

Djogo

Yes, but come back to close the windows and the door.

Tatou meets one of his friends during his break. He is absorbed by the conversation and forgets that he should go back to the workshop. He's seen disappearing with this friend.

Djogo

Tatou left the workshop more than an hour ago. I do not think he will come back. I will try to close shop. First, I need to find out how much I made on this special day.

He opens the box, takes the notes, puts them on the table, and counts:

Ten, twenty, fifty, one hundred thousand francs. Ten, twenty… eighty, one hundred thousand francs. That adds up to two hundred thousand francs! Two hundred thousand francs in one day. Who would have thought? I no longer feel like thinking of my sad past. Long live the work, long live Somo without whom I would have become nothing. If all disabled people were able, like me, to wipe off their tears and work, if the rights of disabled were respected by all, if architects used their creative genius to spare people with disabilities those long stairs which frighten them and threaten them, social integration of this category would become a reality.

Thanks to Somo, my dream has come true. I am no longer a beggar. I am happy. However, I have a mission. I have to be the catalyst for other disabled people. In order to accomplish this, I will ask the Supreme Being:

Make me, Lord!

Make me, Lord, the cane of people with disabilities.

And I will support them.

Make me, Lord, the eyes of the visually impaired.

And for them I will see.

Make me, Lord, the ears of the hearing impaired.

And for them I will hear.

Make me, Lord, the tongue of the voice impaired.

And for them I will speak.

And I will see.

And I will hear.

And I will speak.

For them.

He closes windows and the door, and on this, Tatou arrives. They take a taxi and go home.

END OF EPISODE NINE

EPISODE TEN: Djogo, Somo, Adèle (first candidate), Milo (Adèle's father), Matagne (Adèle's mother), Sokdok (second candidate), Mami Semko (Sokdok's mother), Nouemo (third candidate), Moktomo (Nouemo's mother), Koloko (Nouemo's father), Lele (Nouemo's aunt), Kalassi (a customer), the mayor.

Act 1

Somo and Djogo are at home. They chat.

Djogo
My more-than-brother Somo, I am in the age of maturity and I want to get married.

Somo
Do you have someone in mind for this project?

Djogo
I know an Adèle. We do not have a particular relationship, but I hold her in high esteem.

Somo
In this case, I suggest we go talk about the issue with this girl's family. If she and her parents agree, it is great.

They get ready and go to Adèle's family. She is present as are her parents. Somo knocks on the door.

Milo
Come in!

They go in. Somo and Djogo (together).

Somo and Djogo
Hello to all.

Milo
Welcome, take a seat.

After a few minutes of silence and hesitation from both sides, Somo speaks:

Somo

Our presence here must surprise you. We are here because we saw a treasure in your house and would like to own it.

Milo

What is the treasure?

Somo

Your daughter, Adèle. We wish she were ours, specifically, Djogo's wife.

Matagne

I am in favor, if the two individuals agree.

Milo

Me too, with no problem. Adèle, what do you think about this?

Adele

I am very sorry, but I cannot accept. His body does not move. If we live together, in case there is an aggression, because of his condition he will not be able to defend me. In addition, I am still too young to get married.

Milo

At 23, you think you are too young to get married?

Adele

Yesterday, parents chose the husband for their daughters. Today, the daughters choose. I will not marry him.

With these words, Adèle leaves and goes to her room.

Milo

You saw that we are in favor and the girl involved disagrees. We have to submit to her decision.

Somo and Djogo get up.

Somo

We leave your house empty-handed and with sadness.

Milo

My daughter made her decision. It is a pity. See you next time.

They shake hands and part. Somo and Djogo take a taxi and go back home.

Act 2

A few weeks later, Djogo runs into Sokdok during his stroll.

Djogo

It has been a long time. How are you doing?

Sokdok

Very well. We have not seen each other for ten years. What have you become?

Djogo

I attended training for serigraphy and I opened a private workshop.

Sokdok

I got a bachelor degree in economic sciences. I got into business, as there were no jobs.

Djogo

I am tired of solitude. I would like to know if I could dream of creating a household with you.

Sokdok

You know all too well that for an issue as sensitive as marriage one cannot decide hastily. Give me time to reflect.

Djogo

I hope that the next time we meet you will let me know your decision. I am going to say hi to other friends. See you soon.

Sokdok and Djogo disappear. Sokdok reappears after a few moments at her house, with her mother.

Sokdok

Mother, I ran into an old friend. I would like to marry him.

Mami Semko

Tell me about him a bit.

Sokdok

We were great friends as kids. He is a serigraph. His lower limbs are paralyzed.

Mami Semko

With all the men out there, how can you choose a disabled person as a husband? Do not bring the curse under my roof. Go and find a manager of a company. They keep buying new or used Mercedes, despite the economic crisis. This means they are wealthy.

Sokdok

Thank you for your advice, Mom.

After a few weeks, again during a walk, Djogo and Sokdok run into each other.

Djogo

A few weeks have gone by since we met. What is new?

Sokdok

Nothing, except that I cannot make your dream come true.

Djogo

May I ask why?

Sokdok

The reason is not important. Accept this decision as it is.

Djogo is visibly upset.

Djogo

I am upset by your decision. But since it is made, your will be done. Goodbye.

Sokdok

Goodbye.

Djogo monologues as he gets back home:

Djogo

How can she disappoint me so after having been great friend? Well, that is ok because I know that when God sends a man on the earth, he also sends a woman somewhere for him, and vice versa. Sooner or later, I will meet the girl of my life.

As he continues to monologue, a taxi stops right in front of him. Nouemo gets out of it and hugs him. They are so happy to see each other again after such a long time.

Nouemo

How are you doing, Djogo?

Djogo

Very well. I would say that seeing you, after four years, fills my heart with joy.

Nouemo

Me too. You understand why we say that only mountains cannot meet.

They walk away from the street and find a comfortable spot.

Djogo

Allow me to get into your private life. Did you get married?

Nouemo

No, I am still single. I had a lot of failed love relationships and I reached the conclusion that men are dishonest. I prefer being single, unless I can find a serious friend like you.

Djogo

You cannot state that all men are dishonest. I, too, count some failures in this field. But I am still convinced that it's not good to be alone. If you do not find it objectionable, could we consider a life together?

Nouemo

If you have not changed since I last saw you, I find no objections. However, I need my parents' thoughts on this before I can confirm. You will wait a bit.

Djogo

You will know how to convince your parents on this. I am still the same person you knew long ago.

Nouemo

Have faith in me. Let us meet again in this same spot in two weeks, Saturday at 4 PM.

They hug and go their own way. While going in the opposite directions, they both turn at the same time to gaze at each other, as if they do not feel like parting. At the turn, they disappear. After a few moments, Nouemo is at her house, with her parents.

Nouemo

Mother, I will soon present my future husband to you and Father.

Moktomo

Who is he?

Nouemo

We were great friends as kids. We were separated only a few years ago.

Moktomo

Does he have money?

Nouemo

Mom, love is not contingent upon money. We love each other deeply. What characterizes him is that he is disabled…

Koloko

Stop! Youth today are surprising. In my time, the parents would choose the husband or the wife for their children. That is what made a marriage durable. Now, because of emancipation, everyone thinks all is allowed. In addition, you talk about a disabled. Do you not know that if you marry him, you will have disabled children? They are mystical beings. I do not want to hear you talk about disabled people.

Nouemo

Father, why do you have so many prejudices against a disabled person? I know a few who had children with able-bodied persons and these children are normal and very handsome. I also know a couple who are both disabled and their children are normal. Let us consider them as normal people.

Koloko

Do not insist. I do not need a disabled person in my family.

Nouemo

We do not choose our fate. No one knows what tomorrow will bring. I've made up my mind: I will marry him.

As Koloko nods negatively, Nouemo enters her room angrily, shuts the door, and falls asleep. Two weeks later, the meeting takes place as planned:

Djogo

How are you, Nouemo?

Nouemo

Well, more or less.

Djogo

Why more or less?

Nouemo

Because after the last time we met, I expressed the issue that you know to my parents. My father staunchly opposes our wedding. I am living in anger with him.

Djogo *(in anguish)*

Does it mean that it is not possible?

Nouemo

I've made up my mind. Despite his opposition, we are going to get married. A marriage is an affair between two people, before being an affair of the whole family.

Djogo

In certain cases, the man gets the woman pregnant so that her parents will agree to the wedding. I do not want us to get to that point; that is why I am greatly embarrassed.

Nouemo

We also need to hear your parents' point of view.

Djogo

Well, then, I suggest you come with me to my home. I will introduce you to my guardian, who is all for me.

Nouemo

Let us go!

They take a taxi and arrive. Somo is there.

Djogo

My more-than-brother, Somo, I present to you Nouemo, my fiancée.

Somo

Who?

Djogo

My fiancée.

Somo

I was waiting for this. It is good to be engaged early, because the life expectancy is reduced. I will give you all my financial and material support for the organization of your wedding. Nowadays, it is good to open the engagement and then close it right away so that any foe cannot make the project fail.

Nouemo

That is right.

Djogo

If this depended only on me, we could ask the mayor to celebrate our marriage in two months.

Somo goes to his room and comes back with a bottle of palm wine. All get a glass and chat:

Somo

You want to get engaged. Well, be advised that a roof hides many issues: your dirty laundry needs to be washed within the family and not in public. Otherwise, do not expose your private life in public. Be ready to forgive each other. Communication is very important.

Djogo

I have been with her for about three hours. It would be good for her to go back home now, in order not to be in trouble with her parents.

Everybody gets up to accompany Nouemo. She hails a taxi. Djogo gets back into the house with Somo. Nouemo is now with her parents.

Koloko

Where are you coming from?

Nouemo

I was with Djogo. He introduced me to his guardian and we agreed to get married in two months.

Koloko

What are you saying? I already told you, and I repeat that I do not need a disabled person in my family. Do not count on me for this marriage. Or rather, leave this home.

Under her father's threats, Nouemo leaves the house. She has just the chance to take some clothes and put them in her bag. Far from her house, she monologues.

Nouemo

Here I am, made to leave my home, only because I decided to marry a disabled person. Where am I going to go? Should I go back to Djogo or to my Aunt Lele? …

Nouemo takes refuge at her Aunt Lele's and explains her situation to her.

Good evening, Aunt Lele.

Lele

Good evening. What brings you here at such a late time?

Nouemo

Here is my problem: My father ousted me from home because I decided to get married to a disabled person.

Lele serves dinner to Nouemo before continuing the conversation.

Lele

What is wrong with marrying a disabled?

Nouemo

Nothing. We are planning to get married in two months.

Lele

Where does this disabled live?

Nouemo

Not far from here.

Lele

We shall go see him immediately, and with him, we shall meet with Mother and Father for the arrangements.

They ride a taxi to Djogo's. Somo is not there, but Djogo is busy painting portraits.

Djogo

Welcome, please have a seat.

Nouemo and Lele

Thank you.

Nouemo

I wanted to let you know that my father still opposes this marriage. He sent me away from home. This is my Aunt Lele. She is surprised and upset by my father's position and has offered to play the role of mediator. Let us all go home to convince my father.

Djogo, Nouemo, and Lele take a taxi to go to Nouemo's. Koloko is sitting in the verandah smoking his pipe. When he sees them coming, he becomes furious.

Lele

Good evening, Koloko. Why are you angry?

Koloko

First of all, I demand that this man who is following you go back home.

Djogo

Ehm … Ehm … I …

Koloko

Do not insist. Leave!

Djogo, visibly upset, leaves.

Lele

Well, dear Koloko, I do not understand you. What would you do if your daughter were disabled, or if you were to become disabled?

Koloko

In any case, you can proceed and arrange for the marriage. But do not count on me at any level.

With these words, he leaves, gets into his room, and slams the door. Lele and Nouemo go back and dialogue.

Lele

Prepare your wedding as if nothing happened. He will give in.

Two months passed. One day before the wedding, Djogo enters a boutique to buy his wedding suit. In the boutique, there is another customer who approaches him:

Kalassi

Hello, sir!

Djogo

Good morning!

Kalassi takes a stack of notes from his pocket. In the midst of these notes, he takes 10 francs and offers them to Djogo.

I thank you for the charity. From a roll of over 100. 000 new francs, you took a note for 10 francs to give me! Keep the money and please be advised that I come here to do some shopping, just like you.

Kalassi, feeling ashamed, puts his money back. Djogo buys his suit and goes home. It is their wedding day. Everyone is at the town hall except Nouemo's father and Lele who are arguing at home.

Lele

We are already late and they are just waiting for you.

Koloko

I am not going.

Lele

Avoid a curse that would strike you if you rejected he whom we mistakenly say is among the cursed. Remember one thing: The world of the disabled is a world in which we can easily enter, but we cannot leave. Today, you walk well; tomorrow, a car may hit you and cut off your leg. Frankly, you are already disabled because your age makes you to walk with great effort. Therefore, it is not sin that causes disability.

Koloko

What you said has compelled me to change my mind. May God forgive me. Let us go.

They hail a taxi and drive to the town hall where everyone awaits. Their arrival coincides with the arrival of the mayor. Everyone is happy. The mayor starts.

The mayor

Good morning, everyone. I apologize for being late. We are gathered here today to celebrate the wedding of Nouemo and Djogo. The institution of marriage is very old. The bible says in Matthew 19: 5-6: "A man shall leave his father and mother and be joined to his wife, and the two shall become one flesh. Therefore what God has joined together, let no one separate." Do you, Nouemo, take Djogo as your husband for better for worse...

Nouemo

I do!

Everybody applauds.

The mayor

Do you, Djogo, take Nouemo as your bride for better for worse...

Djogo

Yes, I do!

Everybody applauds. The bride and groom exchange their wedding bands and sign documents.

The mayor
The parents should come sign as well!

All hug, pictures are taken, and Koloko and the bride and groom reconcile. The mayor leaves. After a moment of euphoria, the wedding party moves off and they are seen later at the wedding reception as they are eating, drinking, and dancing.

The END.

www.ingramcontent.com/pod-product-compliance
Lightning Source LLC
LaVergne TN
LVHW041541060526
838200LV00037B/1088